THE LEETER
SPIAKING SINGLISH

1

THE LEETER

SPIAKING

SINGLISH

BOOK 1:
END-PARTICLES

Gwee Li Sui

Marshall Cavendish
Editions

Published in 2022 by Marshall Cavendish Editions
An imprint of Marshall Cavendish International

Other Marshall Cavendish Offices:
Marshall Cavendish Corporation, 800 Westchester Ave, Suite N-641, Rye Brook,
NY 10573, USA • Marshall Cavendish International (Thailand) Co Ltd, 253 Asoke,
16th Floor, Sukhumvit 21 Road, Klongtoey Nua, Wattana, Bangkok 10110, Thailand
• Marshall Cavendish (Malaysia) Sdn Bhd, Times Subang, Lot 46, Subang Hi-Tech
Industrial Park, Batu Tiga, 40000 Shah Alam, Selangor Darul Ehsan, Malaysia

Marshall Cavendish is a registered trademark of Times Publishing Limited

National Library Board, Singapore Cataloguing in Publication Data

Name(s): Gwee, Li Sui, 1970-
Title: The Leeter Spiaking Singlish. Book 1, End-particles / Gwee Li Sui.
Description: Singapore : Marshall Cavendish Editions, 2022.
Identifier(s): ISBN 978-981-4974-74-5
Subject(s): LCSH: English language--Variation--Singapore. | English language--
Spoken English--Singapore. | English language--Dialects--Singapore.
Classification: DDC 427.95957--dc23

Printed in Singapore

CONTENTS

TERIMA KASIH!

WHEN UNKER WAS a boi-boi, my lao peh used to tuition me England. Tuition teacher last time oredi not cheap, and summore my family low SES. My lao peh's England was learn from ang moh one, so it is quite powderful. But hor, when he was not telling me simi past tense lah, present tense lah, future perfect continuous tense lah, he acherly spoke a bit differently. So I got a bit blur.

Only later did I unnerstan this other way of spiaking was called Singlish. When I gave my lao peh a copy of *Spiaking Singlish* some years ago, he asked me where I learnt all this nonsense from. I said, "From you lor." He stunned like vegetable. He thought he only got teach me England! But chewren are liddat mah. We got ears. We pick up what we hear and not what ah laos wan us to know nia.

So the champion I need to thank here is Ricardo Monteiro Gilbert Alphonso Gwee Seng Hong. I previously got sayang a lot of other peepur liao. Those kakis started me on my current ongoing journey to think and write about Singlish. But, with this new phase, I fewl I should hormat the ah pek who began it all in me. He is a true pioneer. And he deen even know it.

INTRODUCTION

SINGLISH IS WHAT AH? Singlish is Singapore's unofficial language. It is *not* its official language. If you anyhowly say and then say I say, I sure kena buak gooyoo one. Singapore's official languages got four: England, Melayu, Mandarin, and Tamil. But this does not make Singlish an underground language since everywhere you go can still hear it. Look at our commercials or even our Gahmen websites and social media – it is oso there. So why liddat?

As the pirate Chow Yun-fat in some filem sagely says, "Welcome to Singapore!" Singlish's status is the tok kong metaphor for this real Singapore that chumchums the lawful and the unlawful, the said and the unsaid, the official and the subversive. Here got the full richness of Sinkie life in all its lawa and gila contradictions. It is where values and ideas get very the

9

messy and the different social layers acherly interact.

In this Singapore, our last time low-crass hawker culture can now become our yaya UNESCO-listed cultural heritage. In it, our leaders of a system that tekans Singlish can somehow be among its kilat speakers. Or consider the Sinkies who always how lian they bilingual or multilingual but, when it comes to Singlish, suddenly cannot. Terbalik got those we dismiss as bo tak chek – but some can spiak a whole range of local languages ler!

You see, the straight truth is this. What many say about Singapore is *neh* the whole reality, nor is, to be sure, what they dun say about it. One day, Singlish sure will tio enshrined as the island's heritage language – but right now no lor. Singlish is what happens when not just Singapore's official languages but hampalang languages and dialects used in it campur. It kapos their words lah, phrases lah, syntaxes lah, and transforms all these with wit and charm.

My this humble book series *The Leeter Spiaking Singlish* is something that more or less re-treads my original *Spiaking Singlish* from 2017. Wah, that one got sell macam hot kalipoks siol! But it has areas that still can make lagi steady such as its structure and its scope. Oso, unker fewls the material covered there needs some updating liao. So this one is same-same but different

– or maybe different-different but same? (Got anyone say liddis?)

I am now arranging my discussion by categories. Each volume got just a few chapters, so easier to digest and follow, but the chapters are oso *longer*, some even double their former lengths. Hampalang content is oso revised lah, boosted lah, and, where need be, corrighted. New chapters sure must have one. The Singlish is cranked up, made lagi heow, because I fewl can liao lah. We can push this summore to achieve more Singlish huats.

The volume in your hands focuses on one sibeh tok kong feature in the spiaking of Singlish. It is the use of end-particles. I got say this many times liao. If you wan to learn Singlish, you can pick up all the funny words you suka – "teh siew dai" lah, "kopi-O kosong" lah, "alamak" lah, "steady pom pi pi" lah. That is a fun chow mugger's way to learn, but dun expect to *sound* authentic lor. To be truly champion, you need to acquire the Sinkie accent.

You must oso know your Singlish end-particles – which, I tell you now, is *fifty per cent* of fluency. Unker no bedek you one. Master these, and you oredi halfway to becoming a solid Singlish speaker. Other Singlish words you may drop here drop there, but use just one end-particle salah and you pecah lobang. Everybawdy will know you wayang king liao. Terbalik, if you spiak perfect England but, as your sentences end, you let slip zhun Singlish end-particles, we will know you Singlish can one. No use kay-kay!

Wait ah. Talk until now you know an end-particle is what anot? Simi sai ah? Well, a particle in any language is a unit that buay sai inflect – that is to say, cannot change to make a new, specific meaning. A noun in England can change from singular to plural by adding an "-s" or "-es", tio bo? A verb can change by switching its tense, corright? So a noun or a verb is not a particle lor. While a particle may ownself not change, it can always link with other words to do this.

An *end*-particle is such a modifier that primarily comes at the end of a sentence or a clause. Its appearance changes the meaning of the whole construction – yes, it is that powderful one! In this book, we will look at a whole bunch of them: "lah", "leh", "ler", "lor", "loh", "liao", "ha", "ah", "hor", "wor", "mah", "meh", "siol", "sial", "sia", "eh", "nia", "neh", and "bah". Some are long-long oredi got use although their uses may have evolved. Others are sibeh new even to my ears!

Got some pandai peepur claim "can", "what", and "one" are oso end-particles, but I dunno leh. "Can" in Singlish still works like an England modal verb what – except, when we ask a question, we can put it in front or behind. So "Can we go kai kai?" and "We go kai kai, can?" are same-same. The case with "what" seems more related to the cow-peh form of "what" while "one" is so much more! Maybe we should talk about all these elsewhere.

I use the term "end-particle" to mark a departure from the normal term "sentence-final particle" cunning linguists got use. It is not to say that they are incompatible hor. Many East and Southeast Asian languages – from Mandarin and Japanese to Indonesian and Thai – got such sentence-final particles one. But I wish to free our Singlish ones from the restrictive senses tied to those. I see Singlish end-particles potentially and oredi doing more.

Flexibility and this freedom to be flexible must maintain for something that, at the centre, is still evolving. Unker is not exaggerating to say that today's Singlish sure will not resemble macam Singlish in fifty years' time. Just compare it now to how ah peks and ah mms remember spiaking when last time policemen wore shorts! So, insofar as we are dealing with a young language, we better get used to multiplicities and transformations lah.

As such, I try not to centralise the question of word origin since usage is negotiate – or we say chum siong – in multicultural societies one. Source informs as anything historical informs, by providing an interesting note, but we cannot confuse it with *application*. Still hor, got some peepur so hung up on original meanings that they forget how language is a living thing. You just cannot turn back the clock to get speakers nowsaday to accept or keep to a set of meanings we no longer relate to lah.

In Singlish, as in any language, words that kena absorbed move away from their source meanings. Consider "goondu", "pok kai", and "shack" lor. These words have long-long gone on a journey of spontaneous transformation. Their uses and speowlings are macam in a dance, can change or, for a while, glance back, gain this meaning that meaning or lose old ones. With "lah", if we focus on its Melayu and cheena senses nia, we will overlook how today it got meanings that dun fall into either. These are come from practical life ler.

Oso, a free hand must mean that words can always come and go. Words circulate as long as they still got their relevance. I may now hear new end-particles such as "bah" as once a pong a time I got hear "dong", "deh", "sih", "siak", and "siot". My discussion here does not mean any end-particle is confirm-plus-chop will last or cannot change summore hor. In fact, one choobi development with regard to old end-particles is that they are becoming *stackable*. Consider "The repairman cabut liao lah!" and "I sappork you mah hor?"

What is going on there siol? Saya tak tahu. Unker listens and writes books nia. I no create anything per se. So this is all I fewl I wan to say in an introduction. If got one thing I hope you can take away, it is this. Monoculture is shiok for clear, zhun meanings and for control over the whole linguistic field. But multiculturalism celebrates flux, ambiguity, and a broad range of meanings. A language *of* a multicultural society can think macam a homogeneous one anot? You say lah.

1

"LAH" YOUR HEAD LAH!

YOU KNOW WHAT IS the problem with Singlish's street cred? Every joker who has ever heard it before thinks he or she can spiak it. Wah piang eh! Just ask that random ang moh who has been in Singapore for a few weeks. You may hear him or her how lian say, "You think I cannot speak Singlish lah?" Ang moh, acherly I dun think you cannot hor. I *know* – because that use of "lah" is sibeh salah.

Poor, poor "lah"! It has kena sai from so many lazy learners that sometimes we wonder maybe we still ang moh colony. Come on lah, show some respect to our Sinkie tongue, can? That line "Is 'lah' a note to follow 'soh'?" not funny liao – we got hear it a gazillion times. Wilful ignorance liddis is not choobi, and yet all these goondus still must ngeh-ngeh lai. "How go to Orchard Road lah?" "Lah your friend is so beautiful." "The chicken rice nice-nice leh lah!"

What the *fiak!* (Yes, that is how to say the F word. "What the fish!" oso can.) "Lah" has to be macam among the most abused words in the history of abused words in the world. One time two times anyhowly nemmind, but dun say you love Singlish and then bo learn properly and keep talking cock. Tuan-tuan dan puan-puan, time we set the rules straight for the sake of all Sinkies' sanity!

First, "lah" is used at the *end* of a sentence or a clause – almost nowhere else. Got one exception, but we will talk about it later. So no "Lah you is so funny" or "I take lah the bus home". This is not French please, you bodoh. But you can say "Heck care him lah, let's go!" or use with a filler like "OK", as in "Please lah, OK?" (By the way, "Please lah" does not involve a request hor. It means "For God's sake" – surplise!)

Second, nonid to use "lah" to end every freaking sentence lah. This point deserves a big aiyoh or aiyoyo, which we let out in dismay, shock, or impatience. One "lah" normally can liao – unless you wan to change the tone or to tneh. To tneh is to whimper. So it makes sense when you rugi money at a casino and tneh to a kawan, "Help me lah! Lend me money lah! Utang you one time nia lah!" Otherwise, tolong dun go "lah, lah, lah", can?

Third, "lah" is not bo meaning one. Dun be that kukujiao who treats it macam some slang form of address like "dude" or "babe" or "my man". You certainly should not say "How are you lah?" when you mean "How are you, *bro*?" For that matter, no "Whazzup lah!" or "Yo lah!" ha. Can peepur dun anyhowly tembak and make Singlish speakers kolaveri until vomit blood?

Our "lah" is in part a Melayu suffix which works as an interjection or a command. So "Itulah" means "That's it" while "Pergilah" means "Go away". This "lah" can oso join with "to be" forms such as "ada" and "ia", creating here "adalah" and "ialah". The most famous Melayu "lah" is the one in Singapore's national anthem "Majulah Singapura" lor. The tok kong composer Zubir Said has the line "Marilah kita bersatu" – which translates as "Come *lah*, let us unite".

But there is another major influence. Cheena peepur oso got a "lah" (啦), which comes at the end and in exclamations too. So someone who buay tahan being suanned may scream "Gòule la!" ("够了啦!"), or "Enough!" I got learn a use from Channel Eight dramas that goes "Tǎoyàn! Bùyào la!" ("讨厌! 不要啦!"), loosely translated as "Disgusting! I dowan!" Often it is tnehing KTV hostesses who say one. This other lineage can explain why "lah" is sometimes speowlt the Pinyin way, as "la".

So the Singlish "lah" is acherly reflect Singapore's cultural diversity wor! The Melayu "lah" softens the tone of a command or a request – although this is less true in Bahasa Indonesia, where counterparts such as "sih", "dong", and "deh" are milder. Meanwhile, the cheena "lah" is impolite and curt, as when we hear "Yea lah!" or "No lah!"… or maybe that oso comes from Indonesia one?

The sheer difference yoked in Singlish's "lah" accounts for why it can be so expressive. It got multiple meanings, and each meaning is defined firstly by the context at play. Depending on its point, "lah" can provoke reactions in listeners ranging from pek-chekness to shiokness. I identify its four main types here:

STEADY LAH!

1. The *pleading* "lah" chuts exasperation. It appears in lines such as "Go away lah!" or "Go and die lah!", oso "Pergi mampus lah!" The last two are just lagi jialat ways of saying get lost.

2. The *emphatic* "lah" is excited, angry, or shocked. You find it in, for example, "You see lah!", which zooms in on you seeing – since, presumably, that is what you *deen* do. The cry means "Look what you did!" or "Deen I say to watch out?"

3. The *affirmative* "lah" is for rah-rah purposes one. It is heard in encouragements such as "Steady lah!" or "Solid lah!", both of which mean "You're amazing! Keep it up!" You can oso say "Siow lah!" – that is, "You're positively mad!"

4. The only "lah" that need not follow the end-of-sentence or -clause rule is the *enumerative* "lah". This "lah" oso neh comes once since it punctuates items in a list of at least two: "This lah, that lah" or "Here lah, there lah." When asked "Where got jamban?", consider saying, "Level One lah, Level Two lah, Level Three lah…"

"Lah" Your Head Lah!

All these "lahs" can oso differentiate by tone. *None* of them involves the singsong "lah" from the filem *The Sound of Music* hor. The pleading "lah" sounds like a deflating balloon: "laaah". Can add vibration for effect. The emphatic "lah" is a spurt ending in a higher pitch, macam when something drops on your foot. The affirmative "lah" is a spurt too, but it pulls downwards after going up, showing the very control of fewling it signals. You can make the enumerative "lah" happy like bird or sian – so long as all instances sound same-same.

So, everybawdy – especially ang mohs – tolong, OK? Dun simi sai oso chut pattern and go "lah" lah. Some of you seriously pattern more than badminton. It hardly ennobles you and, in fact, makes you look stupiak even if you think you very can. Use "lah" must use sparingly and zhun-zhun lah. Study to get it tio. When at last you can, you sure will win over the sibeh easily wounded hearts of Sinkies faster than any HDB upgrading!

2

"LEH" OR "LER" – GOT DIFFERENCE?

TOLONG CAN DUN teach ang mohs "lah" is the easiest Singlish word to use? It is not lor! It is not even a simper end-particle since its meaning changes according to where and how you say it. If you anyhowly whack, you sure will sound like a kukujiao – unless that is your goal, then OK lor. "Lah", like "ha" and "hor", belongs to a class of complex end-particles that dun have one core meaning one. Rather, they are unnerstooded through a mix of context and tone.

The simper end-particles are the rest: "leh" lah, "ler" lah, "lor" lah, "loh" lah, "mah" lah, "meh" lah, and so on. But "leh" and "ler" – like "lor" and "loh" – tend to get mixed up a lot. The two are dangerously same-same but different. One leeter slip at the end, and your listeners blur liao. You can tell your appa on the phone "I can hear you leh", but you say "I can hear you ler" you macam no big no small. You can dismiss an insurance agent with "I got no time ler", but you try with "I got no time leh". Try lah.

Of these two words, "ler" is simper-er to unnerstan. It has one clear meaning that cannot be changed by either tone or volume one. "Ler" just asserts "Dunchoo know?" or "I think you should know". So, when your boss asks you to OT again, you may garang retort, "I three days haven't thng chu to bathe and koon ler." When some Ah Beng beos you but you auntie, you may confess, "Paiseh, I oredi kahwinned ler."

"Ler" is in-your-face and brusque one. It mentions or reveals a truth in part to make its speaker look yaya or saat – that is to say, arrogant or cool. After all, this speaker thinks the fact ought to be apparent mah! At the same time, "ler" malus the addressee, highlighting him or her to be sibeh duh to have to be told. The end-particle draws attention to what someone still needs to be taught, informed, or reminded and so cucuks in a way that does not give face.

In fact, the plain spiaking of "ler" is why it got no variation in meaning. Its very flatness performs its honesty lor. Try intonating for different intentions, and you will learn fast that cannot one! Even if you say "ler" loud-loud for emphasis, for some strange reason, its impact will not grow by any amount. This is why unker calls it simper. It admits to a degree that fewls sarcastic but at least cannot sabo you by implying something else or something more you dun mean.

But this does not mean "ler" cannot stir ah stir different responses ler. Its truth-telling means that it can rip into falsehoods and pretences and jolt their utterers. Hearing "ler" can wake the mind liao. The hearer gabras and, kena caught off-guard, tends to respond with "Ha?", "Ah?", or "Orh".

So, when a politician beams "Wah, I so hansum on TV!", his aide may interject, "You deen zip your pants ler." "Ha? Orh" follows. Then maybe someone will lose a job.

Meanwhile, "leh" is a whole different show of power. "Leh" does not challenge but rather sucks up one. It specifically taps into a feature in our patriarchal society called tnehing. This "tneh" is not pronounced as "teh", as in tea. Must have the nasalised "n" sound. "Tneh" is something from the Ah Beng's Big Book of Love, which describes how his chickadee Ah Lian uses unintelligible sounds to manipulate him and get her way. Yes, it is a kind of manja (not ganja), but the sounds are not choobi. They are often sibeh irritating to hear.

To be sure, tnehing is not just a char bor thing, but men who tneh will kena suanned for being kuniang. A kuniang, from the Mandarin "young lady" (姑娘), is ngeh-ngeh pronounced off-key in Singlish one. It describes being vain, wimpy, or helpless and can be used sama-sama on males and females. So, while an Ah Lian may tneh, it does not automatically make her kuniang. Many Ah Lians – like some Minahs, their Malay counterparts – are sibeh independent one. But some NS boi may tneh to get his buddy to polish his boots, earning the tu lan response, "Why you so kuniang ha?"

"Leh" is this word to tneh with or to make one's spiaking tneh. It whines, pleads, grovels, and quibbles but does not exactly argue a case. In fact, when you use, say, "Panchan leh" to ask for kindness and be let off, you *disrupt* good arguments. In my earlier NS boi example, the kengster's words are likely to be "Buddy, help me polish my boots leh" – said with his face scrunched macam a sad puppy. But got argument or logic here meh? Dun have. Geero.

Rather, "leh" appeals to some subconscious link between friends, relatives, lovers, or – at the most basic level – humans. Yet, unlike "kuniang" and even "tneh", "leh" is not a gendered word at all. It does not hinge on some socialised perception of a weaker sex or some wayang based on it and enabling it. "Leh" is social without being sexual. Its opposite may be the end-particle "ha", which is hostile and confrontational. But "leh" wans pity or tenderness nia.

The commonly used "Dun liddat leh" means "Dun behave this way", where "leh" functions like "please" or "come on". When you are quibbling, you may declare "This nasi lemak cannot make it leh" to register your chow bin. But "leh" helps to soften a request or an objection and can do so in at least three ways. It presents options by a change not in tone but in either length or volume:

1. The *normal* "leh" is mouthed like the rest of a sentence. So you say "Do for me leh" or "You quite stupiak leh" while fewling somewhat paiseh you are saying it.

2. The *long* "leh" goes "leeeeh" to make sure your point is heard in case your hearer is sikit slow from low EQ. This form is truly solid for manja-ing.

3. The *loud* "leh" – or "LEH" – is a buay song command to be taken seriously. It screams "You insensitive or what?" and implies oredi fewling very the hurt.

Sibeh simper, corright? To give in to a "leh" request or grouse, just reply "OK lah" or "OK lor", and you ho say liao! But, to bo hiew, you can act blur or say "Sorry lah", "Cannot lah", or, best, "Siam lah!", "Siow ah!", "Pergi mampus lah!", or any one of Singlish's lawa expletives. Of course, talk logic oso can, but you will soon learn harshness remains the most kilat response. It is one thing to have to refuse someone, but it involves a whole psychological battle to repel an onslaught of tnehing.

3

THE "LOR" AND "LOH" OF IT

THERE ARE SINGLISH end-particles that sound macam related, and they are. I can think of "ah" and "ha" and the triplets "siol", "sial", and "sia" as examples. Then there are those that sound related – but no ler. One case is "leh" and "ler", and another is "lor" and "loh". Even Singlish speakers sometimes anyhowly hentam and use the speowling of one for the other. Lagi jialat is when they utter one even though they mean another. Alamak!

Why liddis ah? It is not like telling them apart is sibeh siong. "Leh" and "ler" can differentiate by how they relate to power. But "lor" and "loh" are about opposing moods. "Loh" got limited use and is primarily for making some announcement lah. You must have a reason to do so one. In this sense, it is acherly closer to "liao" than to "lor". "Unker lai liao!" and "Unker lai loh!" share the same thrill to me, their announcer.

To be sure, "loh" is not like the ang moh "lo" hor. It is not the "loh" of "Lo and behold!" or "Lo, it is I!" You dun say it macam in a magic trick or to yaya papaya – although it *is* about revealing who or what is tok kong. "Loh" is *always* an exclamation. It announces the incredible, whether in joy, uncertainty, or fear. So, when you scream "Siow liao loh!", which means "Great, it's gone bonkers!", it is in no way similar to cow-pehing "Siow liao lor!", which is more "As you see, it's gone bonkers".

The most famous "loh" for Sinkies is in "ORD loh!" or, once a pong a time, "ROD loh!" ORD stands for Operationally Redi Date whereas ROD is for Run-Out Date. These are cries of profound joy every Sinkie male knows in the lead-up to the day he completes his full-time NS. So gerek is this date that, at some point, the SAF decided to change the original "ROD" to "ORD" to remind young men they still got a lifetime of reservist training ahead. (Is my Encik told me one.)

While "loh" may be the least applied of the old Singlish end-particles, "lor" is the most bo power – more so than even "ler"! It is because this one signals

30

resignation. It means that, like it anot, you bo pian, lan lan must go along with something. The content of what is said does not technically make the mood. No matter how kilat or steady a sentence may be, just end with "lor", and suddenly there is a wave of melancholy. You fewl damn sian, damn lembek. "Lor" is liddat one! It betrays your real fewling towards your own words.

So consider my earlier example of "ORD loh!" Someone may scream this, and his bunkmate, who still has a while more to go to smell civvie life, may respond, "Then you book out go havoc lor." Or, lagi curtly, "ORD lor." These retorts are sour grapes, intended to pumchek the gaiety. They accept the case to be happy but choose to play punk or sabo it – because jelly mah. In other words, "lor" is a *dampener*. It is a wet blanket.

BOOK OUT LOH!

We Sinkies know all about being dampened in mood, tio bo? We unnerstan well how, in simi sai we do, however hard we go at it, most things will happen the way they were long-long decided one. No matter how much constructive feedback we may give, it almost always got no effect. Things will run as though on Groundhog Day, macam in a hamster wheel. "Lor" is this product of a sian jit puah culture.

In fact – can I kolaveri summore? – our Gahmen may say we dun hunger and fight hard enough, but that is all talk cock lah. The bare truth is, we kena burnt a lot liao. Say we not productive, and, when we work harder, say we dun spend time with family. Say we not committed to belonging here, and, when we show otherwise, say we got entitlement mentality. Say we should tell our own Singapore stories, and, when we do, hentam us for getting kuai lan.

YOU GO TOUCH LOR.

GWEE

The "Lor" and "Loh" of It

So now we hampalang Sinkies guai-guai lor. You tell us anything, we just say "OK lor". "Lor" is this easy-to-drape word – because it is too resigned to care any further. All possible uses of "lor" revolve around such a fewling of resignation and ways of enhancing it. I can list three main forms here:

1. The *normal* "lor" tends to come with a la-dee-da moral or advice. So, when you say "Now I know lor", you are really showing regret for having believed something before. You are oso warning others against believing too easily.

2. The *aggressive* "lor" is cow-pehed and used often on a stubborn or self-assured fella who is not yet resigned. So, for example, when someone keeps making your job sound senang, you may respond with "Then you do lor!" to invite him or her to a first-hand experience.

3. The *sarcastic* "lor" is meant to create distance from someone who seems to have good reasons not to fewl resigned. So saying "You very smart lor" is not acherly saying "You're very smart" but rather "I guess you think you're very smart"!

"Lor" shows up in several popular phrases such as "OK lor" and "Liddat lor". "OK lor" is said when you wish to signal you are done engaging and cannot be bothered liao. This phrase is inevitable when you talk with bak chew tak stamp peepur – trust me! As for "Liddat lor", it is a stoic utterance. You verbalise it when, say, after many hours spent at baking classes, your cake still tastes like sai (not that I know how that tastes). So how? "Liddat lor."

A once-trending catchphrase has been "Win liao lor". This one is sarky and can be translated as "I guess there's no losing for you". "Win liao lor" involves a situation where some kiasu fella will go to sibeh great lengths to get a favourable outcome. Like when, during lunchtime, a gila babi walks into a hawker centre and chopes with his barang-barang every available seat for his colleagues. He or she may think "Gao tim loh!", but *you* scream with your hands up in the air, "Win liao lor!"

Finally, we have "Die lor". This one you mutter when, say, a day before your family's anticipated trip to Japan, your travel agency suddenly shuts down. You call back but no answer, and mata cannot helpchoo. Fewling pek chek can achieve what? You are as good as dead – so "Die lor". But there is acherly a stage lagi jialat than if you had mati-ed. Sekali you find out your credit card details left with the agency are being used in Russia lah, Slovenia lah, Morocco lah, and a dozen more places, in real time. Liddis siow liao lor.

4

THE MULTIVERSE OF "LIAO"

"LIAO" IS REAL KILAT! It is a versatile Singlish end-particle that agak-agak means oredi or at last. So "Sian liao!" means "I'm long bored!" while "Si liao!" means "It's a goner!" When class time gets too dull, you may sigh, "Sian liao!" When your teacher hears you, your friend may mutter, "Si liao!" ("Mampus!" or "Habis!" oso can.) Then there is the champion "Liao liao!" – where even the "liao" is liao, signalling a confirm-plus-chop end!

"Si liao!" is distinct from "Sudah!" or "Enough!", where you can at least decide *when* to end. When you lose a football game at the void deck, maybe you scream "Sudah!" and thng chu. Later, when your town council puts up notices banning ball games there, it is mampus, habis, liao liao – whether you care anot! This is literally bo liao, and the "liao" is not pronounced same-same as in the other Hokkien "bo liao", which means got nothing better to do. Our "bo liao" is sharp and pulls downwards. It does not swing up.

Oso consider other kilat phrases such as "Siow liao!" and "Lai liao!" You see, "liao" appeals to the Sinkies' lasting love for melodrama and operates on its curve. Blame this on our hopeless TV addiction lor. But, although "Liao liao!" is always set at the end, "Siow liao!" appears elsewhere and simply cannot be said when all is over. "Siow" means crazy, and "Siow liao!" packs a punch. It is dramatic and emotional and sends the mind into a spin.

"Siow liao!" gravitates to a perceived pick-up point in some story, just as things are getting perversely shiok. You use "Siow liao!" *in media res* – that is to say, in the middle of an action you are casting as part of a narrative. (Cheem ah!) You use it when a twist, a climax, or a key confrontation occurs. "Siow liao!" signals how things have gone terbalik or luan and become strangely lagi exciting.

Summore, because "siow" and "liao" rhyme, you get music added to the sensation. Both parts are oso used with unusually hard vowel sounds. A hard "Siow!" – which resembles more the second "siow" than the first in the term "siow-siow" – means "Are you out of your mind?" So tolong hor, you cannot siow-siow go around calling peepur "Siow!" or peepur may, in turn, think you siow.

When the Workers' Party won Aljunied GRC back in 2011, the general cry among Sinkies had been "Siow liao!" Why neh? Because the genius of a GRC had confounded the hopes of oppies since its introduction in 1988. The win broke the stronghold of the powderful PAP not just in Aljunied but oso over the very concept of a GRC. It was the first time the PAP lost one. Jibaboom! That ousting was tok kong. It was a game-changer, a great *plot* twist in our politics.

As for "Lai liao!", while it is oso uttered loud-loud like "Siow liao!", the two are really same-same but different. In fact, they are sibeh distinct, more like opposites wor. The "lai" in "Lai liao!" means come, but, to wan someone to come, you should acherly say "Lai *ah*!" "Lai ah! Lai ah!" – must say twice – is heard a lot at pasar malams and where got freebies to take or tofus to makan.

But "Lai liao!" means something else. It means "Here at last!" and was, in its earliest form, a kind of warning cry. Because, last time policemen wore shorts and hawking was illegal, considerate Sinkies would help look-see look-see for any public health inspector, oso

called ti gu. Once those were spotted, screams of "Ti gu lai liao!" would echo down the streets, and hawkers would kelam kabut kapo whatever they could and cabut.

Today's use of "Lai liao!" is not as fun but still involves our now UNESCO-approved hawker culture. It signals how something expected has come to pass and so marks the end of sianness and speculation. You know, in hawker centres, you need to tan ku ku after you order your char kway teow or rojak, corright? When finally ho liao, the server will shout "Lai liao! Lai liao!", sometimes with sputters of "Siam ah!" or "Sio ah!" I dun think he or she ever uses "Eskew me!", but nemmind. Dun be fussy. Mai hiam.

"Lai liao!", like "Lai ah!", must almost always say twice liddis: "Lai liao! Lai liao!" Dun ask me why hor. Maybe it sounds more musical or can alert the customer to lao nua better? This doubling heightens a fewling of shiokness to prove that, despite the wait, an eventual outcome is mo tak teng. To be sure, the prize can be something desirable or wholly undesirable. What is shiok here lies in *predictability*, in recognising how time or energy has not been wasted.

Indeed, "Lai liao!" has long entered Singapore's political language precisely because our political processes oso can predict one. For example, when a transport minister announces public transport got – wah! – improved, you may hear some cynical snort of "Zhun bo?" But most Sinkies will just diam-diam wait for the other shoe to drop. Our Gahmen is chut pattern type! When news later breaks that bus fare will increase, then the whole jin gang will scream "Lai liao! Lai liao!" to point out "Told you so!"

So, by now, maybe you can guess why I called "Siow liao!" and "Lai liao!" opposites earlier? You see, while both cries are shiok, the fewling behind "Siow liao!" comes from a failure to predict or to manage one. It is buay zai and relates to chaos, to luanness. But "Lai liao!" is about what is *entirely* predictable. Its outcome may take a suspenseful amount of time to happen, but must ai zai, sure will happen one. "Lai liao!" promises pattern.

Both "Siow liao!" and "Lai liao!" are for the drama mama in us Sinkies lah. One shows expectation exceeded while the other shows prolonged expectation gratified. Remember the time when our Gahmen started clamping down on news sites and blogs and we all cow-pehed "Lai liao! Lai liao!" – why ah? Because it was expected mah. But then we went on to oso shout "Siow liao!" since we oso deen know what would happen next or who would kena lim kopi next...

So the next time you check the news, why read in a sian jit pua way when you can go look for patterns, which is sibeh fun? When a MP resigns out of the blue for no apparent reason, you know sure got juicy mangoes liao. Make predictions – issit an affair... or issit an affair? – so that, when the truth is out, you can join fellow Sinkies in the roar of "Lai liao! Lai liao!" Such glorious moments are what brings us closer together even as they make us fewl sikit pandai.

5

HA? AH?... AH!

SAUDARA-SAUDARI, the first thing to get corright about the Singlish "ha" is its pronunciation. "Ha, kong simi?" you may ask. You got hear me anot? There are definite ways *not* to say "ha". You dun say it macam how you respond to a viral video of unkers or aunties fighting: "Ha ha ha!" It is oso not macam how you manage to squeeze into a packed MRT train and yaya go "*Ha!*"

Our "ha" is a long sound – "haaa" – and it slides and curls up in pitch. What is meant is oso determined by how long it is stretched. It can show a wide range of emotions, from wonder or incredulity to condescension and aggression. Sometimes hor, when it is uttered, you may hear it with a silent "h", as "ah". That is more often than not the same thing with French spiakness nia. Let me get to this point first.

To be sure, unker is not saying "ah" is always inter-changeable with "ha" ha. You got a *hard* "ah" and a *soft* "ah". The hard "ah" is can swap with "ha" – as in "You good ah!", which, like "You good ha!", works as back-handed praise. "You good ah!" and "You good ha!" chut same-same positive energy. But the affirmation they give seem to come from a place of unclear sincerity. You dunno how the speaker really fewls inside. Sounds a bit jelly, if not buay song.

The soft "ah" is heard in exclamations such as "Chiong ah!" and "Heng ah!" "Chiong" means charge or rush while "heng" means lucky. The "ah" here is less

43

layered and simply expresses wonder, rapture, or relief. So, at a sale's opening, everybawdy may shout "Chiong ah!" as they push through the doors. Once they are done looting, they may fewl happy like bird and go "Heng ah!" The whole jin gang will then rejoice with a collective "Huat ah!"

Consider how you neh hear peepur cow-peh "Chiong *ha*!" or "Heng *ha*!" or "Huat *ha*!" in any context – which is interesting. Why ah? Maybe because, in such cries, the operative words are oredi front and centre and so exhaust whatever comes after. The real reason saya tak tahu, but the question should oredi prove a basic point for us. "Ha" and "ah" are *not* a total match. You can say "ha" to mean "ah" but not "ah" just to mean "ha". (Ah?)

HERE GOT DOG HA!

The hard "ah" is simply "ha" – got no difference. "Ha" joins an atas class of Singlish end-particles that famously includes "hor". These end-particles got evolve to pop up almost *anywhere* in speech and not at the end of a sentence or a clause nia. They can give pause or stress to what has been mentioned before. Summore, they can point to what is to come as substantial and prepare the hearer for its impact.

So, while it is OK to say "Gopal damn one kind", which sarcastically describes Gopal as one of a kind, you should try saying with some flair lah. Say "Gopal *ha* damn one kind" or "Gopal *ah* damn one kind" – and you will see what got change. You will have isolated Gopal as someone with a mo tak teng talent. But, to lagi sayang Gopal even as you ketuk him, you can say "Gopal *hor* damn one kind".

Between "ha" and "hor", "hor" is generally kinder lah. "Hor" is whiny and gossipy whereas "ha" fewls kuai lan and accusatory. When "ha" early-early appears in a sentence, it is to let you the listener know what or who is the problem so that you can agree with the charge and get worked up sooner. (That is unless *you* are the problem – in which case you got a choice and a head start on how to react lor.)

Of course, like all versatile end-particles, "ha" – for its magic power to show up anywhere – is prone to overuse. Some peepur like to overdo the ha-ing and abuse it for breathing in a rambling speech. So you may hear: "You ha whole day ha sit with kopi watch TV ha dun ha do anything ha and ha now pretend ha you dun hear me ha…" An abundance of "ha" is a confirm-plus-chop symptom of a nag, someone who is compulsively lor sor.

Used just at the end of a sentence, "ha" becomes lagi interesting – if that is possible. It can denote one of several shades of buay-songness differentiated by mere tone. Yes, dun play-play or siow-siow with this hor! "Ha" is serious Singlish stuff and not for la-dee-da ang mohs and yaya kay ang mohs one. Here are six main forms I have observed so far:

1. The *abrasive* "ha" signals a thinly veiled threat. So, in "You dun kacau me ha!", "ha" is a way of saying "I'm telling you" or "I'm warning you" not to be annoying. Push it, and you may tio hoot.

2. The *intrusive* "ha" sounds like the abrasive "ha" but appears in a question nia. It is inquisitive in a way that fewls judgemental and sometimes interrogative macam mata. Thus, in "Where you going ha?", the degree of unpleasantness depends on whether a kaypoh or one's appa, amma, or spouse is asking.

3. The *suspicious* "ha" curls to end on a flat, lower note. It hovers somewhere between a question

and a sceptical opinion. For example, "You very pandai ha?" or "You very smart ha?" means macam "Do you really think you're that smart?"

4. The *deaf* "ha" is a question in itself and can signal disinterest or genuine failure to hear or unner-stan. It starts higher in pitch than the earlier versions of "ha" and simply means "What did you say?" or "What are you saying?"

5. The *un-un-un-un-unbelievable* "ha" is cow-pehed like the deaf "ha" but with greater volume and surprise: "*Ha?!*" It is definitely distinct from the deaf "ha" since what is said *is* heard. It means "What the *heck* am I hearing?"

6. Finally, the *retreating* "ha" is pitched lowest and uniquely winds down without ever curling up, macam a stalled engine. It expresses buay song, lan lan settlement after having been unkind or distrustful, as when a response to a clarification goes "Liddat ha". This means "I see now what you mean".

Let me simplify these summore with a scenario where all six forms can be used in concert:

Amma: You nonid to study ha? (The suspicious "ha".)

Son: Ha? (The deaf "ha".)

Amma: Dun act cute with me ha! (The abrasive "ha".)

Son: So sian, why you so Gahmen ha? (The intrusive "ha".)

Amma: *Ha?!* (The un-un-un-un-unbelievable "ha".)

Son: Errr... OK, study ha. (The retreating "ha".)

6

WORDS AT WAR: "HOR" VERSUS "WOR"

MOST SINKIES WOULD have heard some version of this stupiak joke before. A newly kahwinned man laments how his mother-in-law always comes over to stay. "That lao char bor is an ass siol!" he cow-pehs. His kakis, shocked by his words, retort, "Aiyoh, why you say until liddat?" "It's true lor," he reveals. "Every day I hear her on the phone talk bad about me liddis: 'He hor, he hor, he hor...'"

I got say this was a stupiak joke mah. "Hor" is certainly one buay song end-particle, right up there with "ha". But, while "ha" is stern with a wagging finger, "hor" is more macam a bull's huff. The two same-same chut pek-chekness and require listeners to pay strict attention. So tu lan are they that they got evolve to pop up not just at the end of sentences and clauses but left, right, centre – almost *anywhere*! They very the action one.

By "almost", I mean to admit the earliest spot "hor" and "ha" can appear is still as the second word, neh as the first. They can come after the first noun, pronoun, or noun phrase. So, as much as we may hear "You ha" or "That monyet ha", we may oso hear "That buaya hor" or, as in our joke, "He hor". No "Ha you" or "Hor he" hor (or ha) – because the starting constructions do two things. They highlight who or what is of main concern as well as prepare hearers for this fella or thing to kena tekanded.

The overuse of "hor", as with "ha", is a sure warning of a talker so cheong hei that you may wan to switch off. This yakker does not seem to realise that he or she got overstep some boundary of polite conversation liao. Demands are made and expectations outlined. The spiaking fewls entitled. But where "I tell you ha" and "I tell you hor" differ lies in how the latter *can* be less yaya one. There is room to modulate up or down, according to how well a speaker wans to be received.

Consider hearing a nag go, "Can still gamble hor? You hor better wise up hor!" The three "hors" here are acherly same-same but different. The first one, said in a high pitch, implies an observation. The second can go high or low and arrows blame at someone. The third, most huffish, pulls down and threatens. In fact, all these illustrate for us three main types of "hor":

1. The *naggy* "hor" kiaps to peepur, things, places, and actions that are being assessed. When you hear this form, it means critical thought is being applied to what just precedes it. So a food review may begin with "This mee rebus hor..."

2. The *demanding* "hor" asserts the right to be taken seriously. It may indicate a command or an advice, as in "Everybawdy listen up hor!" It

oso almost always involves an unclear authority which may or may not be its user.

3. The *chaffing* "hor" is the most friend-friend as it welcomes a chat. It presents what is known or observed as a question – for example, "You very thoughtful hor?" This is done so as to get the other to affirm, clarify, or oppose the information.

Now, "hor" and "wor" are neh mixed up by legit Singlish speakers one. But learners of Singlish can confuse – because these two words look and sound sikit alike mah. Unlike with "leh" and "ler" or "lor" and "loh", you suay-suay will not get much sayang for saying one when you mean the other here. As such, you better learn to gostan and corright your word choice before you continue lah. It is really OK. We can tahan that. We just nonid peepur to cannot still ngeh-ngeh lai.

The reason why "hor" and "wor" must say clearly is because they operate in sibeh different universes. A salah end-particle will create the salah enviroment and invite the salah mood lor. If, for example, you say "I suka this makan hor" when you mean "I suka this makan *wor*", your host may think you damn one kind. Lagi worse is if you tell your chewren "Diam wor" when you mean "Diam *hor*" – good luck siol! While the world of "hor" is embattled, the world of "wor" is terbalik sweetness and light.

"Wor" is not exactly same-same as "wah" – exclaimed in wonder or surpise – but I grant there is some link lah. "Wah" *neh* ends a sentence or a clause, and so you cannot anyhowly call it an end-particle. But "Wah, you so pandai!" and "You so pandai wor!" got comparable meaning that can help us unnerstan both words better. (By the way, oso dun go mispronounce "pandai" as "pantat" – unless you are the jelly kind. "Pantat" points to where the sun does not shine. It would not work as praise.)

"Wor" is totally less innocent than "wah", which you must let out with bak chew wide-wide. Meanwhile, "wor" manifests disbelief in an ambiguously positive way. You may sound stunned like vegetable when you say "wor", but this has an inkling that

QUITE FAR WOR.

you think it is all quite kay. So "Your house very cantik wor!" can be read for varying sincerity, depending on how pally-pally the speaker and the hearer are lor.

That said, "wor" is still less complicated than "hor" wor. Linguistically, "wor" got no different ways of saying and different places in a sentence for inserting. It just appears at the end as a way to tell its hearer ham-palang that got said must be unnerstooded as having good intentions. As an experience, "wor" is optimistic but not trusting; it simply acts cute. "Hor" is worldly, practical, and brash.

So you imagine what happens when "wor" and "hor" are used close together lah. Can guess? What happens when an immovable "wor" meets an unstoppable "hor"? Well, in such direct conflict, one will have to surrender control of its meaning to the other. Consider what happens to "wor" in "Pay attention hor. This vase very the precious one wor". Then consider "hor" in "That restaurant super atas wor! I better dress up hor?"

In the first, "hor" sets a context in which how tok kong the vase is becomes part of another thing. It becomes the reason for why you better dun play-play around it. In the second, "wor" establishes the restaurant's high-crass aura. When you go, you better dun sia suay, throw your own face – in this sense, "hor" is repressed by "wor". Opposing natures need not create a contradiction so long as you know how to prioritise lor.

7

THIS IS STILL A TITLE MAH

"MAH" IS NOT for amma or mother, and it is not short for mama, the term for unker in Tamil. Yes, the mama shop at the bottom of your HDB block is belong to your unker one. A mama shop should not be confused with a mamak stall, which is something else altogether. The former refers to a convenience store whereas the latter is an al fresco restaurant serving sedap Indian Muslim makan.

But – aiyoh – I oredi digress. Basically, when a Singlish speaker uses the word "mah", he or she is not invoking his or her lao bu or some middle-aged guy like me, OK? "Mah" is rather another of the simper Singlish end-particles, so ai zai, dun stress. You can chut pattern with "mah" just by adding it to the end of a sentence or a clause, and can liao. The word magically turns everything you have said before into what ought to be obvious.

So, when someone asks why he or she catches no ball when you presumably spiak Singlish, you explain, "You jiak kentang one mah." This translates as "Isn't it obvious you ang moh pai one?" (Did I just translate Singlish into Singlish? Nemmind.) "Ang moh pai" refers to those yaya papayas oredi kena brainwashed by ang moh culture. Maybe, after hearing you, this siow ting tong may still liak bo kiew, but that is not your problem liao.

Or, say, your kakis invite you to tuang with them after work and maybe thani until mabok, but you dowan. You say no, and they ask why no. So you keng a lembek face and clarify, "I pumchek liao mah." This means "Can't you tell I'm oredi knackered?" (Acherly, what you wan to do is thng chu and watch Korean TV drama.) A notti kaki may add to tekan you, "Issit? We deen know you so weak one mah."

To be sure, "mah" has to be pronounced properly or peepur sure will blur one. Dun go on an abrupt, high-pitched, monosyllabic "*Mah!*" hor. That is just you calling your amma in any language. It should first have a long vowel sound kept steady, oon-oon jiak bee hoon, like sheep baaing. You must oso have a bunch of words before you end with "mah" lah. Together with the right *tone*, your hearer should be able to know you dun mean the parental "ma".

But what is this tone? For sure, it must not sound macam some question. It is not take after the Mandarin "ma" (吗) one, so tolong dun suka-suka go "Happy mah?" "Happy mah?" your head – it is "Happy mah." You must say it as though fewling sikit sian or pek chek. You need to show how unimpressed you are with having to say what nonid to say one. The saying becomes brain-numbingly teruk.

"Mah" works rather like a slap that sayangs. It is a gentle reminder to another to – in the words of Phua Chu Kang, that greatest TV character in Singapore, JB, and some say Batam – "use your brain" lah. "Mah" is intellectual and humanising in that it reminds you what you should know if you still got some self-respect. So, when someone complains about being fined jialat-jialat for overdue library books, you can respond with "Walao, it's liddat one mah."

Unlike end-particles like "lah" and "leh", "mah" does not change its meaning with volume at all. You can say soft-soft macam talking to geena or loud-loud macam talking to si geena – got no difference. Some may try to make it sound cute or funny or impatient, but the fundamental meaning stays the same. The two main types of "mah" can distinguish by their contexts instead:

1. The *innocent* "mah" directly responds to a query or a statement. So, when it is observed you always study sibeh hard, you may announce, "Yes, I kiasu chow mugger mah!" – which is very the honest and appreciated.

2. The *sarcastic* "mah" is meant as an indirect, buay song response to what has been said. For example, when your lazy superior who only arrows work asks you why you so bo eng, you say, "My boss sibeh on one mah!" With any luck, she may consider it a compliment although you know I know lah.

That really is all, kawan-kawan. The difference between the two "mahs" is a matter of degree, with the second "mah" naturally lagi intense and tu lan than the first. In this light, it is shiok to point out what acherly changes between them is the whole *nature* of an answer. You are likelier to see the innocent "mah" succeeded by the sarcastic "lah" than terbalik, the sarcastic by the innocent – because "mah" is sensitive mah. It doubles down on engaging goondus and kaypohs with sarcasm.

So, when some kukujiao questions the media love for the swimmer Joseph Schooling, you may begin with an innocent "He won Olympic gold medal mah". But, when this joker goes on and on until you buay tahan, you retort, "*You* oso can win gold medal mah!" The point should be clear now. You state the obvious in one to give the benefit of a doubt that the words are earnest. In the other, you spiak in response to a failure to *accept* the obvious.

In "mah" is therefore an interesting fewling, a pek-chekness with communication that often grips the born-and-bled Sinkie. This may be tied to our high-strung, kan cheong, and kiasu culture where many become quick to tembak and not necessarily to hear, think, or process info. So, short of always having to own-self repeat and repeat, Sinkies seem to have invented "mah" to establish clarity and shame lazy spiaking.

This is how unker is explaining "mah" away anyway. I welcome anybawdy who has his or her alternative theory for it because I is very open-minded one mah. In conclusion, shall we practise pronouncing "mah" corrightly so as not to screw it up? Are you redi? Say this tongue-twister five times before you do anything else: "My mama is the makcik in the mama shop mah." Do eet now. If you can and oso know what talking you, you is steady pom pi pi!

8

TO "MEH" OR NOT TO "MEH"?

"Meh", "ler", "loh", and "wor" are among the simper-est standard Singlish end-particles. Unlike the others, they got one way of spiaking and one way of using nia. They got just one tone, unlike the sibeh complicated "lah" and "ha", while volume alters nothing in their meaning, unlike in "leh" and "nia". Context oso zho bo. It cannot affect what they do in the way it can with, say, "liao" and "mah".

So, while "Balik kampung lah!" can mean a few things, "Balik kampung meh?" means one thing nia. "Balik kampung" is a way of telling someone to go back to where he or she came from, like when some team plays very the lao kui football and you dunno whether to laugh or to cry. You can see how – wah! – this is potentially teruk to its recipient, but, at least with "lah", you can modulate to sound less kuai lan (or more). You can change "ha" to "ah" to sound less hostile.

As for "leh", "Balik kampung leh" is a tolong, an invitation that can acherly become a threat when you say its end-particle loud-loud. "Balik kampung nia" offers the sense of "No big deal" or "Haven't given up!" – oso depends on the last word's volume. What "Balik kampung liao!" means turns on who is saying it and who it is said to. If a match spectator say one, it is a prediction that got no hope liao. If the opposing team say one, it is to cucuk or to maluate. But, if a team member ownself says, then it is an admission of loss. Si liao!

Now look at how mo tak teng "meh" is. "Balik kampung *meh*?" – it is always in question form – simply points out: "Are you sure got so jialat?" It throws into doubt the whole claim that someone got no right to be somewhere doing something at some time. It does nothing else. No matter how heow you get with it – going "meh?", "meeeh?", or "MEH?!" – got anything change? Nothing. Geero.

Observe how it and "wor", which oso offers surplise, are comparable. When you review someone's report and say "You not bad wor!", you mean to sound impressed even as you mean "I can't believe you are this good!" "Meh" is same-same but different. It oso casts doubt but turns it all into a negative. When you say "You not bad meh?" or "You so good meh?", you mean "Are *you* sure you are this good?" or, worse, "Nobawdy will believe you are this good". Just one word and pecah lobang liao. Hampalang comes crashing down!

"Meh" not only strictly appears in a question – must be a rhetorical one – but it oso *neh* appears on its own. You cannot just say "Meh?" in the way you can go "Ha?" or "Ah?" (Acherly, I think "ha" and "ah" are the only exceptions in this case lah.) When someone uses "meh" as a terse non-question and on its own, you can consperm this fella is ang moh pai one. Because only in England then got say "Meh" mah!

Dun believe me? You consider what someone means when he or she says "Meh" lor. Say you how lian show your high-SES tai tai kawan your brand new smartphone and lawa handbag, and she goes "Meh". Means what? It means she is bo chup lor. She cannot be bothered with your kucing kurap barang-barang. What you show her is old news or beneath her. But it hor oso means she jiak kentang one – because a Singlish speaker would have said "Sian"!

The shortest form of meh-ing in Singlish takes two words, as in "Got meh?" or "Really meh?" "Got meh?"

is used to ask a fundamental question of whether something happened or something exists. So, when the blur sotong of a checkout girl asks for money and you tell her you oredi gave her fifty dollars, she may respond with "Got meh?" The typical sarky Sinkie response to this response is this: "God in Heaven lah."

But it is "Really meh?" that most sentences ending in "meh" can be reduced to saying. (Really meh?) So, when your supervisor tells you to zho kang in a certain way and you got your doubts, you may say, "Are you sure it should be done that way?" This is a mouthful, frankly, but England you know lah. Or you can say "Liddat one meh?" or just "Really meh?" "Sure anot?" oso works, but that one different lesson.

"Meh" expresses doubt or disbelief as though peepur are out to con you. True-blue Sinkies sibeh dislike kena tipu by others one. We got an ingrained problem with received information – kum sia to an era of kilat Gahmen campaigns maybe? – and so we no longer innocent liao. We *neh* believe there is free lunch. If you jio us something too good to be true, we will tembak back with "Got meh?", "Really meh?", what have you. (If you bo jio and later we find out, we oso hammer you.)

So a shop that gives out freebies gets us automatically thinking, "So good meh?" We cannot believe that humans, for no legit, self-serving reason, are kind or nice, and thus genuine kindness surplises us – before we arm chio that we gain something. Remember this is the same Asian culture that brings you "double-confirm" since one time consperm is not enough. You *cannot* just trust what you see, hear, read, fewl, touch, or breathe, OK!

"Meh" proves peepur who regard scepticism as an ang moh intellectual tradition talk cock sing song nia. Question *everything* is a deeply Sinkie trait, and you can hear our folks test the fabric of the universe all around, always, with one word: "meh". It is indeed not hard to imagine the following cheem conversation taking place...

Ah Seng: I think Fazilah likes me.

Muthu: You likeable meh?

Ah Seng: She says my Instagram selfie is cute!

Muthu: You cute meh?

Ah Seng: I wan to tackle her!

Muthu: You dare meh?

Ah Seng: Bro, utang you money, can?

Muthu: I got money meh?

Ah Seng: I'll pay you back later lah. You know me!

Muthu: I know you meh?

Ah Seng: You dunno me meh?!

Muthu: You dunno I dunno meh?

Ah Seng: You think hampalang I know meh?

Muthu: You think I think meh?

So the Socratic dialogue goes on.

9

THE TERROR TRIPLETS: "SIOL", "SIAL", "SIA"

WRITING ABOUT "SIOL" is very the siong because this word is sibeh misunnerstooded. Of hampalang Singlish end-particles out there, "siol" is hands down the most controversial siol. Some Singlish speakers will just not use it while others are gong-gong about how to use it. Some say "siol" is Malay peepur's "sia" while others say "sia" is cheena peepur's "siol". But can dun simi sai oso politisai? Slap you one time, then you know!

First off, "siol" is not connected to siol bak chang or hot dumpling ha – because that is "*sio*", you kutu. I mean the "siol" in lines like "Hey, long time no see siol!" or "Your England cannot make it siol!" or "Someone kena buak gooyoo siol!" In all these examples, more may prefer to use "sia", and that one oso can. "Siol" and "sia" seem to do the same thing even though sometimes you hear aksi bodoh peh kambings bedek how there are im-por-tant differences.

But heng unker got do research and go ask these peepur liao. And you know what? *None* of them can say what these differences are or their explanations so koyak until kena sai. So take it from me: "siol" and "sia" are interchangeable, OK. You not happy, form an inter-est group, write a petition, and send to your MP. What is different is more in the hearing sensation than in meaning lah. You can say "Someone how lian got new iPhone siol!" or "Someone how lian got new iPhone sia!" Both pass.

"Siol" and "sia" are used sama-sama to express being taken aback dramatically by disbelief or by envy. So you may be impressed by a recently transferred classmate and say, "That new kid super chow mugger siol!" Or you may be jelly your MP got six-figure salary and you only have a bicycle, so you comment on Facebook, "That kua got two cars sia!" Either end-par-ticle is steady.

By the way, in contrast, "kua" and "ah kua" dun mean the same thing, so check your kolaveri please. "Kua" – from the Mandarin word for melon (瓜), as used in "shǎguā" (傻瓜) – just points to a thick-headed clown. So it is quite safe to call anyone "this kua" or "that kua" in seriousness or in jest: no harm done. Whereas "ah kua" is tied to effeminacy, and it is neh nice to call someone ah kua. So stop eet, you kua!

Where does the word "siol" come from ah? One theory is that it is from the Melayu word "siul", which means to whistle or to poon pee pee. I dunno leh. Unker is very the logical one. If that is the mean-ing, you still will catch no ball when you hear it used when someone cow-pehs, tio bo? Yes, "What talking you siol?" may mean "What the whistle do you mean?" – but what the fiak does *that* mean?

I think "siol" is more a euphemism lah. It may be something said in place of what cannot be said, like how we Singlish speak-ers use "basket" to mean "bastard"

SHIOK SIOL!

and "your kukujiao" to mean... errr... a leeter brudder. No wonder got another theory I sappork which claims "siol" is from trying *not* to say "sial" and tio piaked by one's datuk, nenek, ayah, ibu, pakcik, or makcik. That list means one's grandpa lah, grandma lah, appa lah, amma lah, unker lah, auntie lah, in order.

So the obvious next question is: what does "*sial*" mean? In Melayu, "sial" means damned or damn suay and is a notti, no big no small, hum-tumable word. It is very the likely that "sia" oso came from "sial" since, given how identical they sound, it is logical what! If all this is true, then we have a shiok case where, to siam saying something vulgar, Sinkies have created not one but *two* substitute words. Kawan-kawan, this is how polite and cultured and respectful (some say anal) we are. Boomz!

That "siol", "sia", and "sial" are so alike has not stopped several half past six, homemade experts from trying to buay koyok about fundamental differences. But every time they try, alamak – kua kua. "Kua kua", by the way, oso is unrelated to "kua" *or* "ah kua". It is just an exclamation we use to signal someone or something falling flat on the face and must sayang. See, Singlish sibeh complex one.

Still, some bedek kings ngeh-ngeh argue you can observe positive versus negative uses that differentiate "siol", "sia", and "sial". Aiyoh, unker got observe until cows come home leh – where got? I can say for positive effect "She stylo-milo siol!" or "She stylo-milo sia!" or "She stylo-milo sial!" I can oso say for negative effect "He pumchek siol!" or "He pumchek sia!" or "He pumchek sial!" Hampalang same-same lah, peepur!

Even if we grant that last time might got some differences, it is long-long not the case liao. Terima kasih to how, for generations, we anyhow-anyhow spiak and slur and mispronounce and campur. Now I think it is quite impossible to draw clear lines to tell apart these terror triplets. Meanwhile, older and Melayu-spiaking Sinkies may sumpah one time got even more variants such as "siak" and "siot".

Of the three forms we now use, "siol" remains the kindest on the ear because it is strangely soothing. It may be, like the others, an intensifier, meant to magnify fewlings, but it makes the speaker and hearer rilek most lah. It somehow sounds less harsh than "sia" and "sial" and even choobi! In fact, it may be possible to say that, while all three got the same meaning, yet you may get sibeh different responses depending on which one you use.

Say, when you go pick your kid up at school, you accidentally remark, "Your teacher quite chio siol!" Remark "Your teacher quite chio *sia*!", and your geena may fewl you somewhat low-crass and hum sup. Your wife may get to hear about this. But *neh*, in front of chewren, say "Your teacher quite chio sial!" – because that is... cannot lah! A ti ko may join in with "Uh uh siol", but sekali a parent, another teacher, or, best, the principal oso hears you. Then it is uh *oh* siol.

10

"EH", "NIA", "NEH", "BAH"... WHAT ELSE?

SINGLISH END-PARTICLES are huating! I dun claim to have caught all the ones in play in my leeter book, but I will say I got try my best liao. I go kopitiams lah, void decks lah, polyclinics lah, take buses lah, MRT lah, read online forums lah, random social media posts lah – all for what? Just to kaypoh Sinkie conversations. What I got find, I repork. What I no repork, I no find lor.

Then there are these that notchyet got much for me to say and I oso dunno can kong simi. Their uses are very the basic, and they lack nuances of the kind that lets me call them Singli-fied. Can I suka-suka invent my own word "Singli-fied" – to mean shiok for general Singlish speakers? These end-particles may come in two ways. They either still fewl too tied to their forms in their source languages or are used mostly by peepur who spiak those languages.

Thus, while I consider them more or less kucing kurap, I should still list them here for completeness's sake lah. The oldest of these and yet still minor is surely "eh". "Eh" cannot confuse with the "eh" in "eh sai" hor. Just like the "sai" in "eh sai" cannot confuse with excrement. The term is Hokkien for "can" or "boleh" – or, to be more zhun, "can do" or "can be done". But the "eh" I mean is what we get entirely in short exclamations such as "Walao eh!", "Wah piang eh!", and "Shiok eh!"

"Eh" does not acherly mean anything in particular. It fewls more like a way of bringing balance to an intense emotion. It is a filler word, what is used to pause or to signal a need to pause. But there is another

76

use that got meaning. This is when "eh" addresses some bo name person who can be singled out by a quality. The form here *humanises* – so "siow eh" means "you the crazy one", and "lao eh" means "you the old guy".

Next comes "nia", which means just or only or simply nia. It is not the "nia" in the abusive "chow nia nia", or "lousy so-and-so", or in the name "ah nia". An ah nia is a cantik girl-girl who last time Singlish speakers oso called an anone. Nowsaday, she is either a xiao mei mei – must pronounced off-key from the Mandarin form (小妹妹) – or, if older, a chio bu. You dun say "kuniang" or "missy", OK? "Kuniang" is a feminine con-struct while a missy is a nurse lah.

LIDDIS NIA?

So, when you ask a kawan for money, he may answer, "I got twenty cents nia." This means the amount is all he has. Sounds simper enough – except that "nia" is oso overly tied to its context for sense. It gets horrigibly confusing in view of it always coming at the end of a sentence or a clause nia. So "I love you nia" can mean "I alone love you" or "I love only you". It can oso mean, most teruk of all, "I *merely* love you".

Here is another familiar choobi end-particle: "neh". "Neh" does not mean bro hor. I know got some peepur think it is from the Tamil word "aneh", which refers to a younger brudder, but no lah! (The Tamil for an elder brudder is, by the way, "thambi".) "Neh" is likely again from the cheena dialects and agak-agak echoes the Mandarin "ne" (呢). All these versions are used to signal a question one.

BUT WHERE NEH?

The tok kong difference in the Singlish "neh" is that ours often pops up in sibeh short questions. Consider "Why neh?", "How neh?", "Who neh?", "Where neh?", and so on. "Neh" here serves to stand in for asking the question in full – save energy mah. In this sense, like "nia", it is oso a context-based end-particle that *cannot* be said in abstract one. In abstract, it bo meaning because bo reference.

The baby of the lot must be "bah". I only got hear peepur bah-ing more and more in recent times. This is not related to the baas of sheep, nor is it about calling one's appa. "Bah" is clearly lifted wholesale from the Mandarin "ba" (吧) because it got no imaginative variation from it. It just same-same denotes "let us" or "surely". So "We go makan bah" means "Let us go makan", and "Elections coming bah" means "Surely elections are coming".

In these pronouncements, there should be a sense of sianness with how things stand. The desire is to move on liao, leading to what is said being a decisive push forward. So, in "We go makan bah", the invitation

to us is to mai zho kang and make makan happen. In "Elections coming bah", what is offered up is a means to interpret a series of strange, leeter huats such as all kinds of sappork and rebates rolling out.

Nonid to say, all these end-particles still got a lot of room to develop. "Eh" can increase its range of meanings and uses. With the rest and especially "bah", they may find themselves used by a broader spectrum of Sinkies. Or not. Unker not Nostradamus mah. We simply cannot tell what will find or lose favour among Singlish speakers. We cannot know too what new, extended, or distorted meanings each can acquire as the language stir ah stir.

All we can know is gleaned from the journey oredi made by established end-particles. We know for sure versatility is tied to longevity, and so the popular end-particles are oso the ones that got become mul-ti-faceted in use. It is oso about relevance, what can enable Sinkies to unnerstan and to express specific real sensations and inklings. Simi sai can add colour not just to speech but oso to life always gains traction.

So the fear of certain languages overwhelming Singlish is bo basis lah. First, hampalang Singlish words are open to be altered and transformed anyway. Second, because relevance is tok kong, words that cannot kiap to Sinkie fewlings sure will ownself drop out one. You can only force words that far into a language. Longevity will still depend on decentralised speakers. Will any of these end-particles evolve to overcome their current limitations? It is hard to tell. Saya tak tahu. But watch with me lah – it is shiok!

~~GROCERY~~ GLOSSARY

Hampalang Singlish words and phrases used in this book are listed here. Those with more than one entry mean they are completely different terms with just the same speowling. Words originating in other languages are given Singlish definitions nia.

ACHERLY: actually
ACT BLUR: act clueless
ACT CUTE: try to be funny
ACTION: energetic; showy
AGAK-AGAK: roughly
AH BENG: uncouth Chinese boy
AH KUA: effeminate man

Glossary

AH LAO: adult; senior
AH LIAN: uncouth Chinese girl
AH MM: old woman
AH NIA: winsome girl
AH PEK: old man
AI ZAI: keep cool
AIYOH: a groan
AIYOYO: a groan
AKSI: overbearing
ALAMAK: oh dear
AMMA: mother
ANEH: younger brother
ANG MOH: white person
ANG MOH PAI: Westernised class
ANONE: cute girl
ANOT: or not
ANYBAWDY: anybody
ANYHOW-ANYHOW: anyhow
ANYHOWLY: anyhow
APPA: father
ARM CHIO: quietly pleased
ARROW: assign work or responsibility to
ATAS: superior; uppity
AUNTIE: middle-aged woman
AYAH: father

BAK CHEW: eyes
BAK CHEW TAK STAMP: clueless
BALIK KAMPUNG: go home; get lost
BARANG-BARANG: belongings
BASKET: bastard
BEDEK: bluff
BEDEK KING: compulsive liar
BEO: hit on
BEST: most extreme
BLUR: clueless; confused
BLUR SOTONG: clueless or confused person
BO: without
BO CHUP: uninterested
BO ENG: too busy
BO HIEW: disregard
BO JIO: fail to invite
BO LIAO: no more
BO LIAO: waste of time
BO PIAN: without choice
BO TAK CHEK: uneducated
BODOH: fool
BODOH PEH KAMBING: stupid goat
BOI: boy
BOI-BOI: little boy
BOLEH: can
BOOMZ: an excited exclamation

BORN AND BLED: born and bred
BRUDDER: brother
BUAK GOOYOO: punished
BUAY KOYOK: tout fake cures
BUAY SAI: cannot; not allowed to
BUAY SONG: disgruntled
BUAY TAHAN: can no longer tolerate
BUAY ZAI: not in control
BUAYA: crocodile; flirt
BURNT: hurt (past participle)

CABUT: run away
CAMPUR: mix
CAN: capable; good enough
CAN DUN: can you not
CANNOT MAKE IT: substandard
CANTIK: pretty; lovely
CATCH NO BALL: cannot understand
CHAMPION: standout
CHAR BOR: woman
CHEEM: profound
CHEENA: Chinese
CHEONG HEI: long-winded
CHEWREN: children
CHIO: stunning
CHIO BU: beautiful woman

CHIONG: charge

CHIONG AH: a battle cry

CHOOBI: adorable

CHOPE: reserve

CHOW BIN: displeasure

CHOW MUGGER: disgustingly diligent student

CHOW NIA NIA: lousy so-and-so

CHUM-CHUM: mix

CHUM SIONG: negotiate

CHUT: emit

CHUT PATTERN: resort to tricks

CIVVIE: civilian

CONFIRM-PLUS-CHOP: guaranteed

CONSPERM: confirm

CORRIGHT: correct

COW-PEH: shout

CUCUK: taunt

CUM: and

DAMN ONE KIND: in one's own league

DATUK: grandfather

DEEN: didn't

DIAM: keep quiet

DIAM-DIAM: quietly

DIE LOR: this is hopeless

DOUBLE-CONFIRM: re-confirm

DOWAN: don't want

DRAMA MAMA: someone who overreacts

DUH: dull-witted

DUN: don't

DUN LIDDAT: don't behave this way

DUN PLAY-PLAY: don't fool around; don't underestimate

DUN STRESS: don't get stressed out

DUNCHOO: don't you

DUNNO: don't know

DUNNO WHETHER TO LAUGH OR TO CRY: unsure how to react

EARLY-EARLY: at an early stage

EET: it (emphasis)

EH SAI: can; allowed to

ENCIK: warrant officer

ENGLAND: English

ESKEW ME: excuse me

EVERYBAWDY: everybody

FEWL: feel

FEWLING: feeling

FILEM: film

FRIEND-FRIEND: friendly

GABRA: panic

GAHMEN: government

GAO TIM: settled

GARANG: brave

GEENA: child

GEERO: zero

GEREK: awesome

GILA: crazy

GILA BABI: unreasonable swine

GIRL-GIRL: girl

GIVE FACE: regard another's feelings

GO AND DIE: get lost

GONG-GONG: ignorant

GOONDU: idiot

GOSTAN: reverse

GOT MEH: did it happen

GRC: Group Representation Constituency

GUAI-GUAI: obedient

HABIS: finished

HALF PAST SIX: lackadaisical

HAMMER: whack

HAMPALANG: all

HANSUM: handsome

HAPPY LIKE BIRD: chirpy; contented

HAVOC: revel; wild

HDB: Housing Development Board
HECK CARE: ignore
HELPCHOO: help you
HENG: lucky
HENG AH: a cry of relief
HENTAM: whack
HEOW: wild; immodest
HIGH CRASS: high class
HIGH SES: high socio-economic status
HO LIAO: ready
HO SAY BO: how are you
HO SAY LIAO: good to go
HOOT: beat up
HORMAT: salute
HORRIGIBLE: horrible and incorrigible
HOW LIAN: boast
HUAT: gain; prosper
HUAT AH: a wish for success
HUM SUP: lecherous
HUM-TUM: whack

IBU: mother
ISSIT: is it

JAMBAN: toilet
JB: Johor Bahru

JELLY: jealous

JIAK KENTANG: Westernised

JIALAT: terrible

JIALAT-JIALAT: a serious extent

JIBABOOM: an explosion

JIO: invite

KACAU: irritate

KAHWIN: marry

KAI KAI: go out for leisure

KAKI: buddy

KALIPOK: curry puff

KAN CHEONG: anxious

KAPO: grab

KAWAN: friend

KAWAN-KAWAN: friends

KAY ANG MOH: Westernised person

KAY: fake; wannabe

KAY-KAY: pretend

KAYPOH: busybody; meddle

KELAM KABUT: panic

KENA: get

KENA SAI: get shat on

KENG: feign a condition

KENGSTER: skiver

KETUK: knock

KIAP: clasp

KIASU: afraid of losing

KILAT: excellent

KOLAVERI: rage

KONG SIMI: what do you mean

KOON: sleep

KOPI: coffee

KOPI-O KOSONG: coffee without milk and sugar

KOPITIAM: coffeeshop

KOYAK: damaged; inferior

KTV: karaoke lounge

KUA: fool; clown

KUA KUA: a sigh of disappointment

KUAI LAN: rascally

KUCING KURAP: insignificant

KUKUJIAO: idiot; rascal

KUM SIA: thank you

KUNIANG: feminine

KUTU: louse

LA-DEE-DA: casual; oblivious

LAGI: even more

LAI: come

LAI AH: come one, come all

LAI LIAO: it is here

LAN LAN: grudging

LAO: old

LAO BU: mother

LAO EH: you old person

LAO KUI: humiliating

LAO NUA: drool

LAO PEH: father

LAST TIME: long ago; at one time

LAST TIME POLICEMEN WORE SHORTS: once when life was different

LAWA: gorgeous

LEETER: little

LEFT, RIGHT, CENTRE: everywhere

LEGIT: legitimate

LEMBEK: flaccid

LIAK BO KIEW: cannot understand

LIAO LIAO: the end

LIDDAT: like that

LIDDAT LOR: it is what it is

LIDDIS: like this

LIM KOPI: face interrogation

LONG-LONG: long ago

LOOK-SEE: survey

LOR SOR: naggy

LOUD-LOUD: loudly

LOW CRASS: low class

LOW SES: low socio-economic status

LUAN: out of control; chaotic

MABOK: drunk
MACAM: like
MAI: refuse
MAI HIAM: no need to be fussy
MAKAN: food; eat
MAKCIK: aunt; middle-aged Malay woman
MALU: embarrass; embarrassing
MALUATE: embarrass
MAMA: uncle
MAMA SHOP: convenience store
MAMAK STALL: street Indian Muslim food stall
MAMPUS: die
MANJA: pampered
MATA: police
MATI: die
MELAYU: Malay
MINAH: Malay girl
MISSY: nurse
MO TAK TENG: incomparable
MONYET: monkey; troublemaker
MRT: Mass Rapid Transit

NEH: never
NEMMIND: never mind

NENEK: grandmother

NGEH-NGEH: persistently

NO BIG NO SMALL: rude; disrespectful

NOBAWDY: nobody

NONID: no need

NONID TO SAY: obvious

NOTCHYET: not yet

NOTTI: naughty

NOWSADAY: nowadays

NS: National Service

OK LOR: if you say so

ON: hardworking and motivated

ONCE A PONG A TIME: once upon a time

OON-OON JIAK BEE HOON: smooth sailing

OPPIES: the opposition

ORD: Operationally Ready Date

OREDI: already

ORH: OK; I see

OSO: also

OT: work overtime

OWNSELF: on one's own

PAISEH: sorry; embarrassed

PAKCIK: uncle; middle-aged Malay man

PALLY-PALLY: on friendly terms

PANCHAN: pardon; give chance

PANDAI: clever

PANTAT: anus

PAP: People's Action Party

PASAR MALAM: street market

PATTERN MORE THAN BADMINTON: attempt a lot of tricks

PECAH LOBANG: wreck a scheme

PEEPUR: people

PEK CHEK: frustrated

PERGI MAMPUS: get lost

PIAK: slap

PLAY PUNK: mess around

PLEASE LAH: for God's sake

POK KAI: broke

POON PEE PEE: whistle

POWDERFUL: powerful

PUMCHEK: exhausted; deflated

RAH-RAH: visibly supportive

REALLY MEH: are you sure

REDI: ready

REPORK: report

RILEK: relax

ROD: Run-Out Date

RUGI: lose

SAAT: cool
SABO: sabotage
SAF: Singapore Armed Forces
SAI: shit
SALAH: wrong
SAMA-SAMA: similarly; together
SAME-SAME: alike
SAME-SAME BUT DIFFERENT: superficially alike
SAPPORK: support
SAUDARA-SAUDARI: brothers and sisters
SAYA TAK TAHU: I don't know
SAYANG: love; cherish; empathise with; wasteful
SEDAP: delicious
SEKALI: what if
SENANG: easygoing
SHACK: extremely tired
SHIOK: amazing
SI: die
SI GEENA: brat
SI LIAO: this is doomed
SIA SUAY: be an embarrassment
SIAM: move aside
SIAN: bored; boring
SIAN JIT PUA: considerably bored
SIAN LIAO: I am bored
SIBEH: very

SIKIT: a little

SIMI: what

SIMI SAI: whatever matter

SIMI SAI OSO POLITISAI: politicise anything and
everything

SIMPER: simple

SINKIE: Singaporean

SIO: piping hot

SIONG: tough

SIOW: crazy

SIOW EH: you crazy person

SIOW LIAO: it has gone bonkers

SIOW ON: irrationally or excessively motivated

SIOW TING TONG: lunatic

SIOW-SIOW: fool around; thoughtlessly

SOFT-SOFT: softly

SOLID: outstanding

SPEOWLING: spelling

SPEOWLT: spelt

SPIAK: speak

SPIAK: flamboyant

STEADY: impressive

STEADY POM PI PI: well done

STIR AH STIR: provoke

STUNNED LIKE VEGETABLE: dumbfounded

STUPIAK: stupid

STYLO-MILO: stylish
SUAN: taunt
SUAY-SUAY: unfortunately
SUDAH: I am done
SUKA: like
SUKA-SUKA: as one pleases
SUMMORE: some more
SUMPAH: swear; promise
SURE ANOT: are you sure
SURPLISE: surprise
SWITCH OFF: tune out

TACKLE: woo
TAHAN: endure
TAI TAI: rich housewife
TALK COCK: talk nonsense
TALK COCK SING SONG: talk nonsense
TAN KU KU: wait for a long time
TEH: tea
TEH SIEW DAI: tea with less sugar
TEKAN: pressure
TEKANDED: pressured (past participle)
TEMBAK: shoot
TERBALIK: the other way round
TERIMA KASIH: thank you
TERUK: nasty; tough

THAMBI: older brother

THANI: consume alcohol

THNG CHU: go home

THROW OWN FACE: embarrass oneself

TI GU: public health inspector

TI KO: lecher

TIO: get

TIO BO: am I right

TIPU: trick; cheat

TNEH: whimper; whine

TOK KONG: important

TOLONG: a plea for help

TU LAN: exasperated

TUAN-TUAN DAN PUAN-PUAN: ladies and gentlemen

TUANG: hang out

TUITION: give tuition; tutor

UH UH SIOL: I freaking agree

UN-UN-UN-UN-UNBELIEVABLE: extremely difficult to believe

UNKER: middle-aged man

UNNERSTAN: understand

UNNERSTOODED: understood (past participle)

UTANG: owe

VERY THE: very
VOID DECK: vacant ground floor of a HDB block

WAH: a cry of wonder
WAH PIANG EH: for goodness's sake
WALAO: for goodness's sake
WAN: want
WAYANG: staged performance
WAYANG KING: expert faker
WHACK: beat up; apply
WHAT TALKING YOU: what do you mean
WHAT THE FIAK: what the f**k
WHAT THE FISH: what the f**k
WHOLE JIN GANG: everyone involved or affected
WIDE-WIDE: very wide
WIN LIAO LOR: you are unassailable

XIAO MEI MEI: little girl

YAYA: arrogant; aloof
YAYA PAPAYA: arrogant person; show off
YOU KNOW I KNOW: this is an open secret
YOU KNOW LAH: I don't need to go on
YOU SAY LAH: you tell me
YOUR HEAD: an expression of disagreement

Glossary

ZHO BO: do nothing

ZHO KANG: work

ZHUN: accurate

ZHUN BO: is this reliable

ZHUN-ZHUN: accurately

ABOUT THE AUTHOR CUM ILLUSTRATOR

Gwee Li Sui suka write lah, draw lah, talk cock sing song lah. He got publish many kilat books from poetry books and comic books to critical guides and lite-ra-ry anthologies. You got buy any of those? Bo, corright? That is why he must now oso make Singlish books lor. Other than *Spiaking Singlish*, he got translate world classics into Singlish, such as Antoine de Saint-Exupéry's *The Leeter Tunku* and Beatrix Potter's *The Tale of Peter Labbit*. This unker sibeh siow on one!